BOOK D

We can use the computer!

Rachel Biheller Bunin
and
Maureen Berliner Engeleit

SCHOLASTIC INC.

Welcome!

Senior Vice President, Director of Education: Dr. Ernest Fleishman
Editorial Director: Mickey Revenaugh
Project Director: Sandy Kelley
Vice President, Director, Editorial Design and Production: Will Kefauver
Cover: Type by Glenn Davis; illustrated by Peter Fasolino
Assistant Production Director: Bryan Samolinski

Design and Art Direction: Ned Campbell, Bill SMITH STUDIO
Designer: Christine Sergi, Bill SMITH STUDIO
Illustrators: Bernard Adnet, Keith Bendis

No part of this publication may be reproduced in whole or in part, or stored in a retrieval system, or transmitted in any form or by any means, electronic, mechanical, photocopying, recording, or otherwise, without written permission of the publisher. For information regarding permission, write to: Scholastic Inc., Classroom Magazine Division, 555 Broadway, New York, NY 10012-3999.

Copyright © 1994 by Scholastic Inc.
All rights reserved. Published by Scholastic Inc.
Printed in the U.S.A.
ISBN 0-590-49545-3
6 7 8 9 10 34 99 98

contents

What is a Computer? 4
- What Does a Computer Do? 5–6
- Input...Processing...Output 7
- Hardware 8–9
- The Keyboard 10–12
- The Mouse 13–14
- Monitors and Printers 15
- Software 16
- Tool Software 17
- Graphical User Interfaces: GUIS 18
- *Review:* Name It! 19

What is Word Processing? 20–21
- The Cursor 22–23
- Tabs and Indents 24–26
- Fonts and Points 27
- Editing a Document 28–30
- Copying and Pasting Text 31–32
- Searching and Replacing 33
- Saving and Printing 34
- *Review:* True or False 35

What is Desktop Publishing? 36
- Terms You Need to Know 37
- Designing a Travel Flier 38–39
- Writing a Travel Flier 40
- Graphics for Your Travel Flier 41–42
- Drawing Tools 43
- Resizing Text and Graphics 44
- *Review:* Word Jumbles 45

What is a Database? 46–47
- Using Fields to Plan Your Trip 48
- Adding Fields to a Record 49
- Records in a File 50
- Sorting by Letter 51
- Sorting by Number 52
- Queries 53
- *Review:* Choose and Use 54

What is a Spreadsheet? 55–56
- The Worksheet 57–58
- Cell Addresses 59
- What if? 60–61
- Functions 62
- Data as Pictures: Graphing 63
- *Review:* Spread the Answers 64

Glossary .... Inside Back Cover

What is a Computer?

A COMPUTER is a machine that works with information. Circle all the machines that you think are computers.

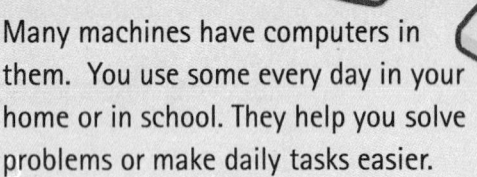

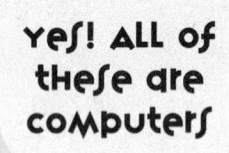

Yes! All of these are computers

Many machines have computers in them. You use some every day in your home or in school. They help you solve problems or make daily tasks easier.

Draw a circle around the machines that you think have computers in them.

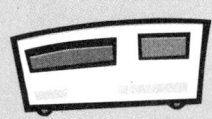

VCR

globe

Nintendo

microwave

book

remote control

Good work! Of course, books and globes are not computers even though they can help you solve problems.

What Does a Computer Do?

A COMPUTER works with `data`. Data is information you put into a computer. Data can be numbers, words, or pictures. A computer stores data in its `memory`. Computers with more memory can store more numbers, words, or pictures than computers with less memory.

desktop computer

telephone

remote control

The data that you give the computer is called `input`. Input is the numbers, words, or pictures that you put into the computer.

Which computer do you think has the most memory?
_____

Yes, a desktop computer has more memory than a TV remote or a telephone because it has to work with a lot more data.

Here are some computers you have probably used. What do you think the input is for each one?

The input for a telephone is _____
_____.

The input for a Nintendo game is _____
_____.

The input for a TV remote control is _____
_____.

The input for a desktop computer is _____
_____.

What is a computer?

Computers work on, or `process`, the data to solve problems. Computers can do things over and over again and never get tired or bored.

Put a ✔ next to those things that you might find tiring or boring to do:

☐ Count to 10

☐ Count to 1,000,000,000

☐ Write a letter to your friend

☐ Write a letter to everyone in your school

☐ Find out if your town has a street called Main Street

☐ Find out how many towns in the United States have a street called Main Street

All those boring or tiring things would be simple tasks for any computer.

The instructions that a computer uses to process data are called `programs`. People write these programs. There are special programs that solve special problems.

The `CPU` is the part of the computer that does the processing. What do you think the letters CPU stand for?

_____ Clear Pink Umbrellas

_____ Classy Purple Umpire

_____ Central Processing Unit

_____ Computer Party Uniforms

right!

When you have worked on a computer, you may want to save what you have done. You can store your work on a disk. Disks that you can take out of the computer and hold in your hand are called `floppy disks`.

When a computer finishes processing the data, you get `output`. Output is what the computer puts out when the job is done.

Input
Processing
Output

Using a computer needs only three simple steps:

1 input is the data that you give your computer to work with.

2 processing is the work that the computer does on the data.

3 output is the answer, or what comes out.

Now let's see if you can figure out the input, processing, and output for these everyday things.

Machine	input	processing	output
1 typewriter	blank paper	typing	typed letter
2 sharpener	_____	sharpening	sharp pencil
3 oven	batter	baking	_____
4 toaster	_____	toasting	_____
5 blender	_____	_____	milk shake
6 sewing	material & thread	_____	_____

Try making up your own:

7 _____ _____ _____ _____

8 _____ _____ _____ _____

What is a computer?

Hardware

WHAT is `hardware`? Hardware is any part of the computer that you can touch. It is hard, so it is called hardware. If it were wet, you might call it wetware. But computers are hard, so we call them HARDWARE.

There is special hardware that lets you get the words, numbers, or pictures into the computer. These are called `input devices`. See if you can match the picture to the description of each device. Write the correct word under the picture.

1 The `keyboard` has a whole lot of keys on it. These keys are buttons. Each key has a letter or number or symbol or little word on it. By pressing on these keys, you tell the computer what to do.

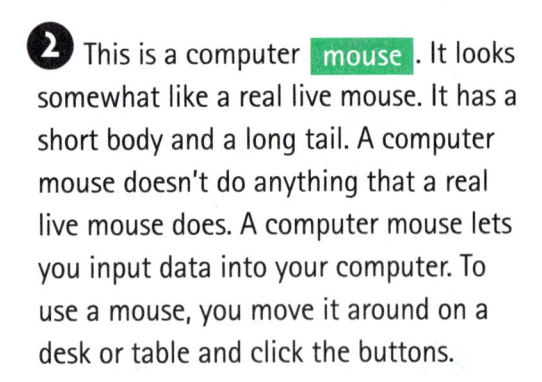

2 This is a computer `mouse`. It looks somewhat like a real live mouse. It has a short body and a long tail. A computer mouse doesn't do anything that a real live mouse does. A computer mouse lets you input data into your computer. To use a mouse, you move it around on a desk or table and click the buttons.

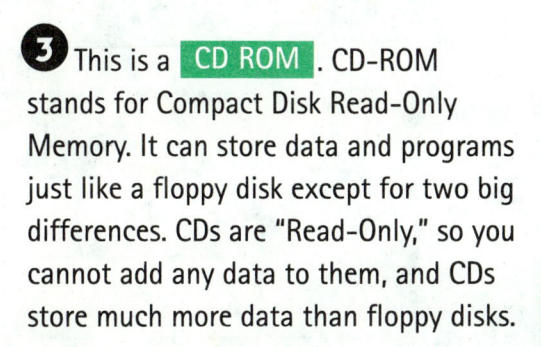

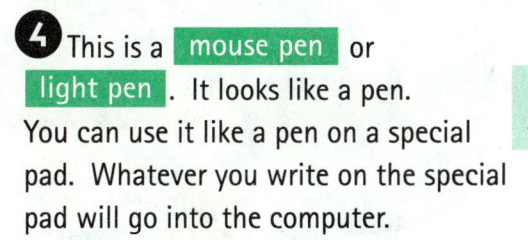

3 This is a CD ROM . CD-ROM stands for Compact Disk Read-Only Memory. It can store data and programs just like a floppy disk except for two big differences. CDs are "Read-Only," so you cannot add any data to them, and CDs store much more data than floppy disks.

4 This is a mouse pen or light pen . It looks like a pen. You can use it like a pen on a special pad. Whatever you write on the special pad will go into the computer.

5 This is a scanner . It reads words, pictures, or numbers on a page and changes them into a form that a computer can understand.

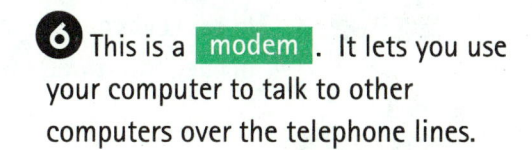

6 This is a modem . It lets you use your computer to talk to other computers over the telephone lines.

What is a computer?

the Keyboard

THIS is a keyboard. You really have to learn keyboarding if you are going to use a computer. Each key is like a button, and you have to press the keys to `key` input into the computer.

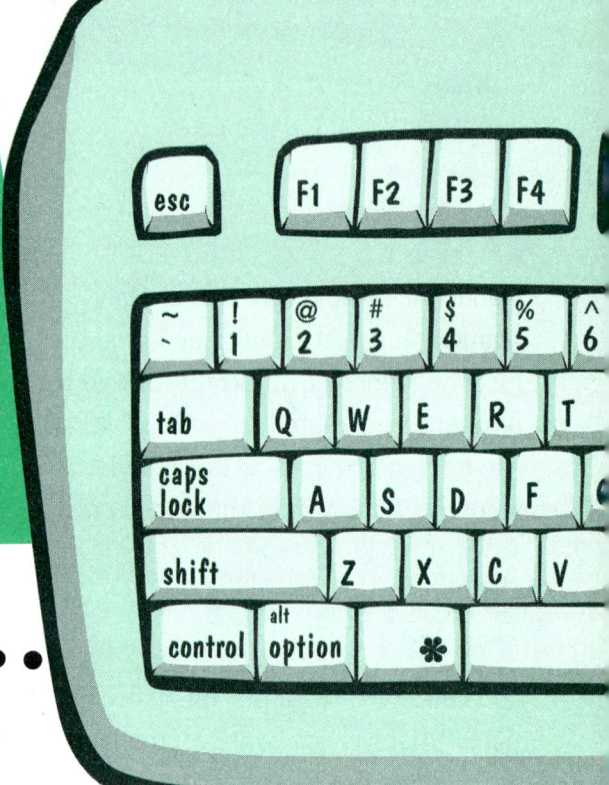

Look at the keyboard. Find the 26 letter keys that are in the middle, divided into three rows.

1 Which 10 letter keys are in the top row?

_____

2 Which 9 letter keys are in the middle row?

_____

3 Which 7 letter keys are in the bottom row?

_____

4 Write your full name.

_____

5 On the picture of the keyboard, draw a circle around each key that has a letter that spells your name.

6 Draw a big circle around all the number keys.

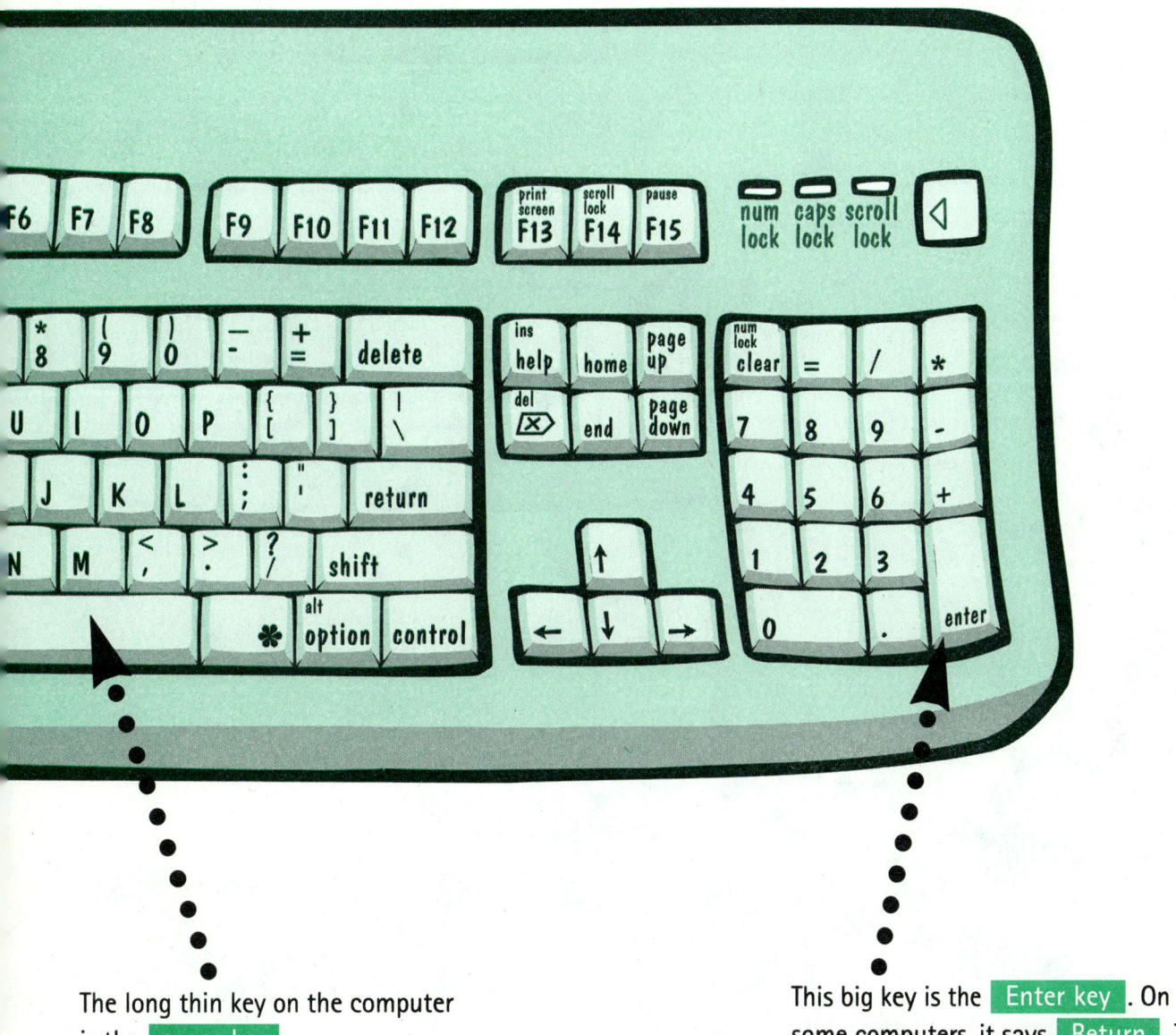

The long thin key on the computer is the space bar .

What do you think this key does?
_____
_____

This big key is the Enter key . On some computers, it says Return . The Enter key is very important. It lets you move to the next line when you are keying words into a computer. It is also the key that you press when you want the computer to do something. You ENTER a command into the computer with the Enter key.

11

what is a computer?

This is the shift key. This key does nothing by itself. You have to press the shift key and a letter key at the same time to make a capital letter.

Write your name again using CAPITAL LETTERS.
_____

The shift key has another VERY IMPORTANT job to do. Look at the keys below.

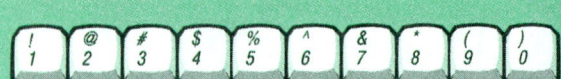

All these keys have two symbols on them. To key in the symbol at the top of the key, you have to press the key and the shift key at the same time. For example, if you want to key an *, you press the [8] key and the shift key at the same time.

For each item below, fill in the symbol that would be keyed.

1. shift 1! = _____
2. shift 6^ = _____
3. shift 2@ = _____
4. shift 7& = _____
5. shift 3# = _____
6. shift 8* = _____
7. shift 4$ = _____
8. shift 9(= _____
9. shift 5% = _____
10. shift 0) = _____

This is the Escape key.

What do you think the ESC key does?
_____
_____

Yes, indeed! When you need to get out fast, you press escape! The ESC key will back you up or get you out of most commands in most programs. It is a handy key to use when you feel trapped or stuck in part of a program.

the Mouse

THIS is a computer mouse. You learned that the computer mouse is an input device.

You push the mouse along a desk or on a pad next to the computer. When you look at your computer screen, you will see an arrow or shape or picture. This is the `cursor`. It tells you where the next letter, number, or symbol will appear on the screen.

Cursors come in many shapes and sizes. Sometimes a cursor is just a small line like this . The cursor often blinks. In some programs, your cursor will be a rectangular box like this □. The cursor tells you where you are on the screen.

When you use a mouse, the cursor on the screen will move exactly the same way you move the mouse. This is called `pointing`.

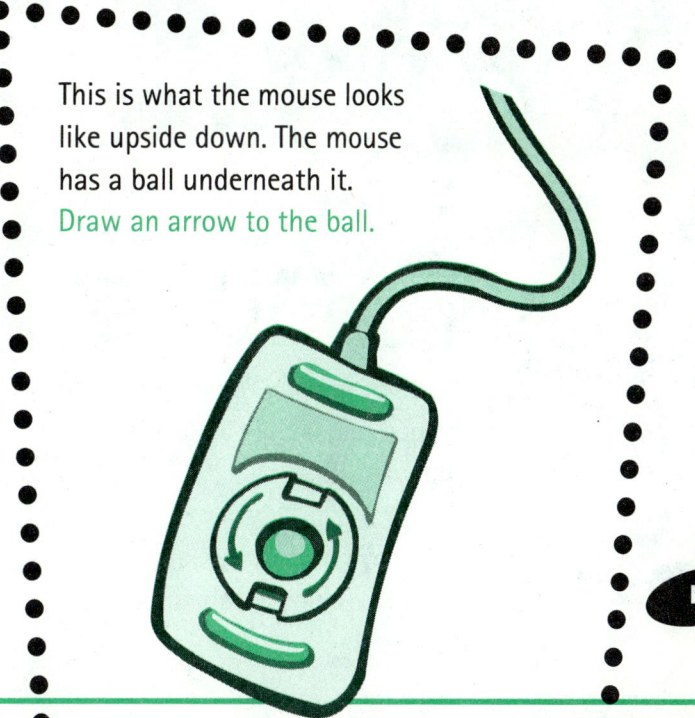

This is what the mouse looks like upside down. The mouse has a ball underneath it.
Draw an arrow to the ball.

What is a computer?

Find the buttons on the top of the mouse in the picture. Sometimes a mouse will have one button, sometimes two, and sometimes three. This mouse has two buttons.

1 Put a big letter **L** in the left mouse button.

2 Put a big letter **R** in the right mouse button.

The left mouse button is really important. It works like the Enter key. You can press the button or `click` to tell the computer what to do. You can `drag` an item around on the screen if you place the cursor on that item and hold the mouse button down. The mouse will drag an item until you let go of the button.

The right button on a mouse often tells the computer to stop doing whatever it was doing. It is a quick way out of a command or action. You just learned about a key on the keyboard that does the same thing as the right mouse button. Do you remember what the key is called?

_____

For each item below, put the mouse action in the correct place. Mouse actions: DRAG, CLICK, POINT, ESCAPE

1 _____ by moving the mouse along the pad to get the cursor where you want it.

2 _____ by pressing the left mouse button to tell the computer what to do.

3 _____ by pressing the right button to get out of a command.

4 _____ by holding the mouse button down as you move the mouse around the pad.

14

Monitors and Printers

Now you know all about input devices. What about getting the data out of the computer? There are two common ways to get your data out. These **output devices** are monitors and printers.

The **monitor** is the screen that is part of your computer. It is like a television screen. That's why a monitor is often called a **screen**.

Some computers have color monitors and display your output in color. Other computers can only show your output in shades of one color. When you key in letters, you will see them on the monitor.

You can have the computer print your output on paper. A **printer** will take the output from the computer and make a **hard copy** on paper.

Unscramble the letters on each computer screen column and print the words on the printer column. The first one is done for you.

1. TNAAIOVC → VACATION
2. RTIP → _____
3. LATRVE → _____
4. EOHTL → _____
5. STUCISEA → _____

What is a computer?

Software

REMEMBER when you learned about hardware? That was easy. Hardware is hard. Software is a bit trickier. Software is not soft. It is not hard. You can't touch software. Software is the programs that tell your computer what to do.

Let's go back to

Input ┈┈┈┐
　　　　　↓
　　　Processing
　　　┈┈┈► Output

Which of the three steps do you think software does?
_____

Correct! Software does the processing. It takes your input and turns it into output. The games you play and the programs that teach you new and interesting things are software.

The operating system is what makes the computer run. It tells the computer which program to run and how to store your data in an organized way. You can think of the operating system as the police officer of the computer.

store counting program on disk!

put part of balloon picture back!

go get drawing program!

print the work order now!

Write the letters OS next to those things you think the operating system can do.

☐ paint a picture　　☐ select which program to run

☐ save a file to a disk

☐ play a chess game

16

Tool Software

TOOL SOFTWARE does all those boring tasks that we mentioned earlier. There are many types of tool software that you can use on your computer. The type of software you need depends on the job you want to do.

Draw a line to connect the software to the output.

Word processing software works with words to help you write letters, notes, or anything that you could write with pen and paper.

Desktop publishing software takes the words that you write and places them on pages with pictures and fancy lettering. You can publish newsletters, newspapers, or books by using this tool.

Graphics software lets you create art on your computer.

Database software helps you organize and keep track of lists of data.

Spreadsheet software helps you add, subtract, multiply, and divide numbers so that you can analyze data.

Communications software helps you talk to your computer from far away and lets your computer talk to other computers.

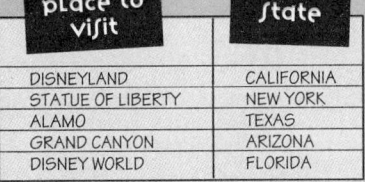

	Cell Address	is for column	and row
1	A1	A	1
2	B12		
3	Z100		
4	FF25		
5	L256		

place to visit	state
DISNEYLAND	CALIFORNIA
STATUE OF LIBERTY	NEW YORK
ALAMO	TEXAS
GRAND CANYON	ARIZONA
DISNEY WORLD	FLORIDA

What is a computer?

Graphical User Interfaces: GUIs

HOW do you tell the computer what to do? You use `Graphical User Interfaces` or `GUIs`. Let's call them "gooeys" for short.

GUIs use pictures or graphics to help you tell your computer what to do. The pictures are called `icons`. The icons look like what you want to do. You use the computer mouse to point and click on the icons.

GUIs also use pull-down menus to help you tell the computer what to do. A menu looks like this:

| FILE | EDIT | FONT | HELP |

You can use your mouse to point and click on menus. Using a mouse you can drag or "pull down" the menus to get more choices. If you pull down the FILE, you get this:

FILE	EDIT	FONT	HELP
NEW			
OPEN			
SAVE			
PRINT			
QUIT			

Look at these icons. The little pictures will tell you what these icons do. On the line, write what each icon does.

✂ _____

_____ 🖨

🗑 _____

_____ 🖌

🔦 _____

What do you think these choices do?

_____
_____
_____
_____

Name It

Word List

click	mouse	Enter key
monitors	process	input
printers	drag	point
hardware	output	software

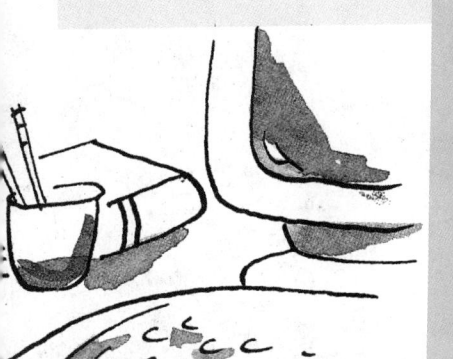

Choose words from the word list to fill in each blank.

1 The parts of the computer that you can touch are called _____.

2 When you give a computer information, it is the _____.

3 Computers take and _____ data to solve problems.

4 When the computer has solved the problem, you get the _____ to look at.

5 Two output devices are _____, which look like TVs, and _____, which give you your output on paper.

6 A _____ is an input device that you roll on a desk or pad to move the cursor on the screen.

7 The button on a mouse is like the _____ on the keyboard.

8 To use a mouse you have to _____ and _____ or _____ to tell the computer what to do.

9 The programs that run the computer are the _____.

19

What is Word Processing

YOU are going away on a trip. All your friends ask you to write to them while you are away. They want to know about your travels and adventures. How can you possibly write to all your friends and still have time to have adventures? Aha! You can take your portable computer with you. Then you will be able to use your word processing skills to write letters to all your friends.

Word processing is more than just keyboarding. When you use word processing, you can write one letter and then edit it for each of your friends. That way, each friend will get a personal letter without your having to write each one from the beginning.

There are special words that you need to know in order to do word processing. The letters, numbers, and all the special signs that you see on the keyboard are called characters . Characters make up the words, or text , of what you key in. The text is called a document .

When you key in a document for the first time, you say you are creating a document .

Underline each activity if you think word processing would make the task easier.

1. Write a letter to one of your friends.

2. Write a letter to twenty of your friends.

3. Pack your suitcase for a two-week trip.

4. Make a checklist of things to pack for a trip.

5. Plan an itinerary of where you will be going.

6. Pack your car for the trip.

7. List the things in your car that should be checked before you make a trip.

8. Telephone the hotels where you will be staying to confirm your room reservations.

9. Write a journal during your trip.

10. Draw pictures of the sights and the people you will meet during your trip.

Now that you understand which tasks you can use word processing for, let's see how it works.

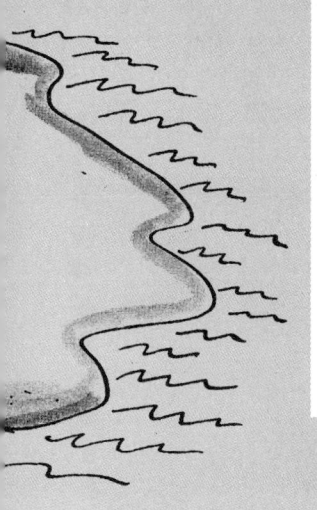

What is Word Processing?

The Cursor

SUPPOSE you are in a new shopping mall and want to have a snack. You don't know where the food is. What do you do? You look for a map of the mall. On the map you see a restaurant. But where are you? You look for the little colored square that says "YOU ARE HERE."

That little colored square is like a `cursor` on a computer. The cursor is a place holder. Sometimes it appears as a blinking line. As you key in characters, the cursor moves along the line to show you where the next character will appear.

You can also move the cursor around by using the arrow keys or the mouse.

The cursor is the square around the "D" in the first line of the letter on the opposite page. Follow the directions below and place a square around the character the cursor would be on.

1. Press the [↓] 2 times.
2. Press the [→] 5 times.
3. Press the [↓] 8 times.
4. Press the [→] 4 times.
5. Press the [↓] 6 times.
6. Press the [↑] 3 times.
7. Press the [←] 4 times.
8. Press the [↓] 5 times.

Dear Tanya,

We have been in the car forever. All we have seen for two days is corn. Sitting on the hump between Emily and Michael is no more fun than sleeping in the same motel room with them. Oh, they really aren't so bad. But if I have to listen to any more Raffi tapes, I think I will scream. Good thing you let me borrow your Game Boy cartridges.

Yesterday, Mom and Dad finally told us all the places we are going to. Take a look at this list. This is going to be one long car trip.

- Sioux Falls, South Dakota
- Rapid City, South Dakota
- Cody, Wyoming
- Teton Village, Wyoming
- Salt Lake City, Utah
- Reno, Nevada
- Yosemite, California
- Los Angeles, California
- Las Vegas, Nevada
- Grand Canyon North, Arizona
- Bryce Canyon National Park, Utah
- Durango, Colorado
- Salina, Kansas
- St. Louis, Missouri
- Columbus, Ohio

I miss home a lot. Don't forget to feed my fish.

Your friend,

what is word processing?

Tabs and Indents

You can use the arrow keys to move your cursor around space by space. But suppose you are keying in columns of numbers? You may want to move the cursor more than one space at a time. Then you use the `Tab` key. When you create a document, you can decide how many spaces will make up one tab.

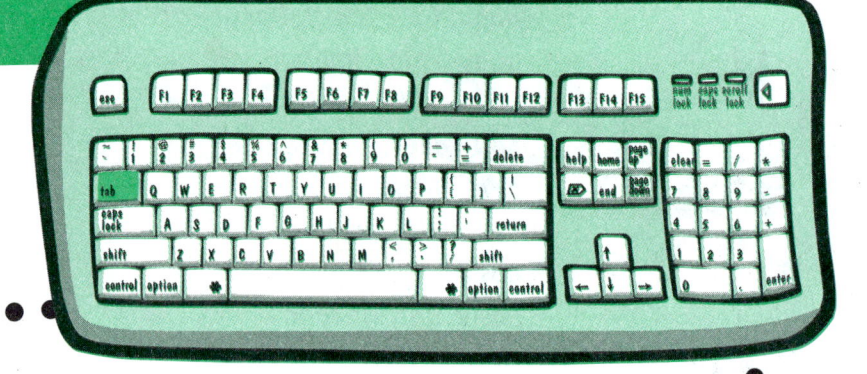

Tab = 5 means that the Tab key will move the cursor 5 spaces to the right. The spaces look like this -----. Now it is your turn. For each item, draw in the spaces or fill in the number that each Tab is equal to.

1 Tab = 2

2 Tab = ☐ -------

3 Tab = ☐ ----

4 Tab = 9

5 Tab = 12

6 Tab = ☐ -----

24

This line was keyed in using the Tab key first. See how the letter "T" is `indented` five spaces from the margin?

But suppose you want to indent the whole paragraph. An indented paragraph catches a reader's attention. Would you have to press the Tab key at the beginning of every line? OF COURSE NOT! Remember, you are using word processing. Different word processing programs have different ways of giving the `Indent` command.

the travel game

1. Get 20 index cards.
2. Write TAB on 16 cards.
3. Write INDENT on the other 4 cards.
4. Shuffle them and put them face down.
5. Trace a traveler playing piece from the top of page 26, and cut out your tracing.
6. Get one die.

good Luck!!

How to play

You need two people. The youngest person rolls the die. The number rolled is the number of spaces the TAB will be for the game. Each person takes turns picking a card. If you pick TAB, move that number of spaces around the outer circle. If you pick INDENT, move to the inner circle. Continue picking cards and moving until someone picks another INDENT card and moves to the HOME circle. The first to get HOME is the winner.

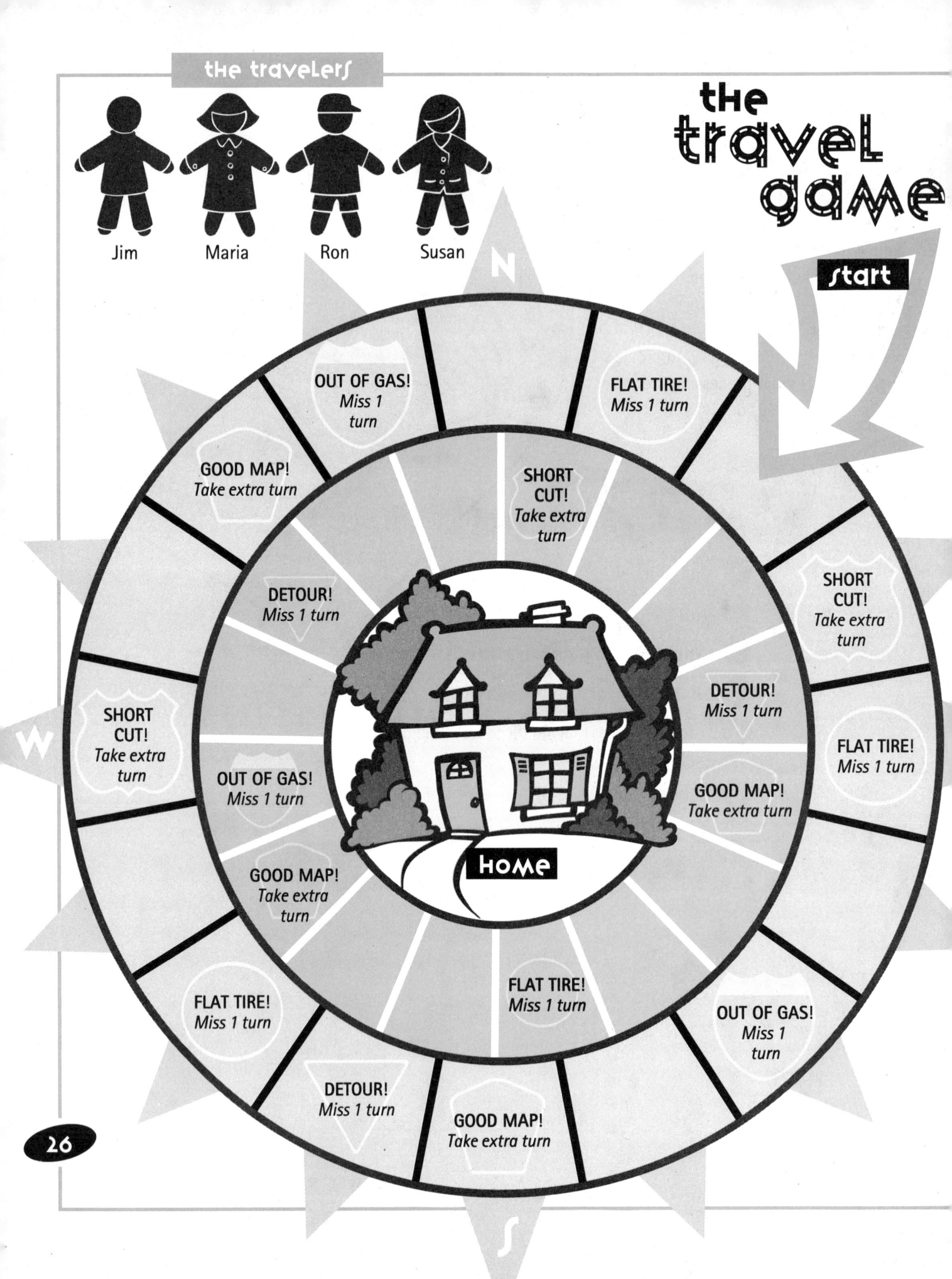

the travelers

Jim   Maria   Ron   Susan

the travel game

start

OUT OF GAS! Miss 1 turn

FLAT TIRE! Miss 1 turn

GOOD MAP! Take extra turn

SHORT CUT! Take extra turn

SHORT CUT! Take extra turn

DETOUR! Miss 1 turn

DETOUR! Miss 1 turn

SHORT CUT! Take extra turn

FLAT TIRE! Miss 1 turn

OUT OF GAS! Miss 1 turn

GOOD MAP! Take extra turn

GOOD MAP! Take extra turn

Home

FLAT TIRE! Miss 1 turn

FLAT TIRE! Miss 1 turn

OUT OF GAS! Miss 1 turn

DETOUR! Miss 1 turn

GOOD MAP! Take extra turn

N   W   S

26

Fonts and Points

YOU can make your letters home look special by changing the style of the letters that you use. **STOP NOW!** Did that get your attention? These different styles of type are called `fonts`. Each font has a name.

Make your own font to match the mood of each word below the line.

_____   _____
     Tired   Scared

_____   _____
     Happy   Silly

A `point` is a measurement of how big the font will be. The larger the number, the bigger the characters. The larger the characters are, the fewer of them will fit on a line.

Below is a word shown in different point sizes. Under each size is a ruler. Count how many characters fit into an inch.

❶ ADVENTURE
|—————1—————2—| ☐ characters fit into an inch

❷ ADVENTURE
|—————1—————2—| ☐ characters fit into an inch

❸ ADVENTURE
|—————1—————2—| ☐ characters fit into an inch

Editing a Document

what is Word Processing?

YOU have written your first letter to your best friend. But what about the rest of your buddies? You know that Ruth is not interested in the same things as your softball teammates. What to do? You can edit by deleting, inserting, and copying and pasting text. Let's begin editing the first letter that you wrote.

deleting text

First, you want to take away the sentence about feeding your fish because only Tanya is taking care of them. To take away a character or a group of characters, you must `delete` them. You can delete by pressing the arrow keys in the direction of the mistake until the cursor reaches the character to be deleted.

If you have a mouse, just point to the character you want deleted and click. When the cursor is in the correct position, press the `Delete` key. The character disappears, and the remaining characters on the screen rush in to fill its space. You can keep pressing the Delete key until you have taken away all the characters that you don't want.

Here is the sentence from the letter. The square is the cursor. It is in the right position to delete.

> I miss home a lot. ▢on't forget to feed my fish.

If you press the Delete key, your sentence will look like this.

> I miss home a lot. on't forget to feed my fish.

To delete the rest of the word *Don't*, you would have to press the Delete key four more times. (With some computers, you put the cursor at the end of the word and backspace to delete each letter.)

Now it's your turn. For each item below, the cursor is on the first letter of the word to be deleted.

In the box at the end, write how many times you would press the Delete key to delete the word.

1. New York, [N]ew York, it's a wonderful town.

2. Carry me back to old [V]irginia.

3. [C]alifornia, here we come.

4. Gary, Indiana, Gary, [I]ndiana, my home, sweet home.

5. [O]klahoma, where the wind comes sweeping down the plains.

6. The stars at night are big and [b]right, deep in the heart of Texas.

7. I left my heart in San [F]rancisco.

8. Off we're going to shuffle, shuffle off to [B]uffalo.

9. [C]hicago, Chicago, I'll see you around.

10. I'm going to Kansas City. Kansas [C]ity, here I come.

inserting text

what is word processing?

WHEN you deleted characters, the remaining text on the line moved closer together. When you `insert` characters, the old characters make room for the new ones. You move your cursor, using the arrows or pointing and clicking with your mouse, to the place on the line where you need to insert the text. Then you key it in. Watch all the other characters move over.

On the right below is a letter with blank spaces. DO NOT LOOK AT IT YET!! Cover it with a piece of paper now. First fill in your own words in the blanks on the left. In case you've forgotten, here's a reminder of what adjectives and nouns are.

An **adjective** describes something or someone: *pretty, hard, smooth*.

A **noun** names a person, place, or thing: *tourist, hotel, film*.

Fill in the blanks with the words called for. Then insert your words into the letter at the right. Draw a cursor, a rectangle, around the first letter of the word you are inserting.

1. name of friend: _____
2. amusement park: _____
3. noun: _____
4. adjective: _____
5. noun: _____
6. noun: _____
7. plural noun: _____
8. your name: _____

Dear _____,
                    1
Yesterday we finally stopped driving. We reached
_____. A theme park is fun to visit on
        2
a hot summer _____ . There are
                    3
lots of _____ things to eat like hot
            4
dogs, pizza, and cotton candy. After you are stuffed
like a _____ , it is time to go on rides.
            5
The roller coaster is sure to make your
_____ feel calm. I wish you could
        6
have seen everything. I will show you
_____ when we get home.
        7
    Your friend,

    _____
        8

30

Copying and Pasting Text

YOU have been traveling in the car for weeks now. Can you believe it? You know every single word to the song "Clementine." You want to write the words in your letter to Aunt Janice. The bad part is that the song has many verses. The good part is that the words to the refrain, repeated between each verse, are the same. You will be able to use the `copy and paste` commands in your word processing program. This is how you do it.

1 Move the cursor to the first character you want to copy.

 [O]h my darling, Clementine oh my darling, oh my darling

2 Highlight all the words that you want to copy.

 | Oh my darling, Clementine oh my darling, oh my darling |

3 Press the `Copy` command key. Your words have not moved yet. This is what you will see now.

 | Oh my darling, Clementine oh my darling, oh my darling |

4 Move the cursor to the place where you want the words to be inserted.

 Oh my darling, Clementine oh my darling, oh my darling

5 Press the `Paste` command key and TA DA!

 Oh my darling, Clementine oh my darling, oh my darling

 Oh my darling, Clementine oh my darling, oh my darling

What is Word Processing?

Highlight the refrain by drawing a box around it. Then draw a cursor (a rectangle) at each spot where the refrain should be copied.

Verse 1   In a cavern, in a canyon, excavating for a mine,
           Dwelt a miner, forty-niner,
           And his daughter, Clementine.

   Refrain   **Oh my darling, Clementine oh my darling, oh my darling**
              Thou art lost and gone forever
              Dreadful sorry, Clementine.

Verse 2   Light she was and like a fairy,
           And her shoes were number nine,
           Herring boxes, without topses,
           Sandals were for Clementine.

   Verse 3   Drove she ducklings to the water,
              Every morning just at nine,
              Hit her foot against a splinter,
              Fell into the foaming brine.

      Verse 4   Ruby lips above the water,
                 Blowing bubbles soft and fine,
                 But alas, I was no swimmer,
                 So, I lost my Clementine.

Searching and Replacing

YOU finished typing that whole letter to Aunt Janice. You look at the screen and realize that you have a problem. You mixed up some of the words in the refrain. And the mistake occurs all through the song since you used the copy command to insert the refrain between all the verses.

By now you know that word processing will have a command to help you solve the problem. It is a command called `Search and Replace`.

When you begin to search and replace, the computer will ask you what characters you are searching for. After you enter them, the computer will ask you what characters you want to replace them with. Here is how it works with "Clementine":

SEARCH FOR: Oh, my darling, Clementine oh my darling, oh my darling

REPLACE WITH: Oh, my darling, oh my darling, oh my darling Clementine

Look back at pages 31 and 32. Draw a circle around each line on those pages that the computer would search for and replace.

what is Word Processing?

Saving and Printing

You have finished writing a letter and naturally you want to print it out so that you can mail it. But first you have to `save` your document.

Try to give your documents names that tell what they are about. Document names should also be short. Many computers only allow up to 8 characters for a name. For some computers, you cannot use spaces in a document name.

Here is one document name you might use: LETTZACK. The letters LETT tell you that the document is a letter, and the letters ZACK tell you that the letter is to Zachary.

Then press the `print` command key. The computer will ask you which file, or document, you want to print. Enter the file name and press Enter.

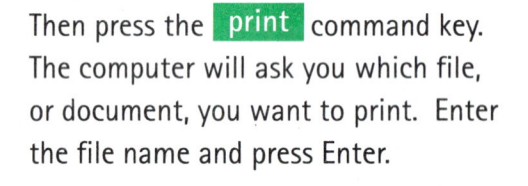

Here are descriptions of some documents.
Circle the best document name to print each one.

1 Letter to the softball team.
PRINT FILE: a. LETTFLY b. FLYBAL c. LETTTEAM

2 Letter to Uncle Richard.
PRINT FILE: a. LETTUNC b. TRIP c. AIRPLANE

3 Letter to your teacher, Mrs. Smith.
PRINT FILE: a. SMITH b. LETTEACH c. CLASS

True or False

Read each sentence. Decide whether it is TRUE or FALSE, and circle your answer.

1 Different styles of type are called fonts.
TRUE   FALSE

2 If you wanted to add a new sentence to a letter, you would copy and paste.
TRUE   FALSE

3 When you save a document, you try to name it after your older brother.
TRUE   FALSE

4 When you add characters or text, you are inserting them.   (TRUE)   FALSE

5 Letters, numbers, and special signs that are on the keyboard are called characters.
TRUE   FALSE

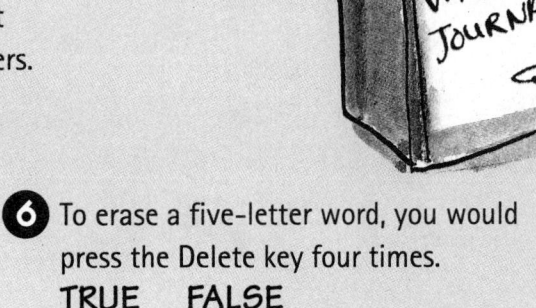

6 To erase a five-letter word, you would press the Delete key four times.
TRUE   FALSE

7 To correct the same mistake throughout a 10-page letter, you would use the search-and-replace command.
TRUE   FALSE

8 You can move the cursor by using the arrow keys or by pointing and clicking the mouse.   TRUE   FALSE

9 The Tab key moves the cursor one space at a time.   TRUE   FALSE

10 When you type a document for the first time, you say you are editing a document.   TRUE   FALSE

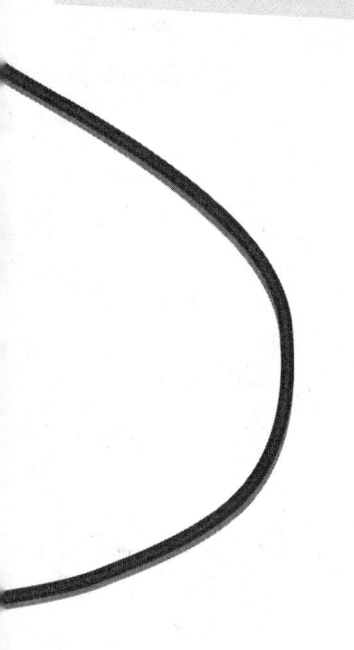

What is Desktop Publishing?

DESKTOP PUBLISHING software is a computer tool that is used to make the newspapers and magazines that you see every day. When you see words and pictures, or `text` and `graphics`, together on a printed page, it is likely that desktop publishing was used to design and make it.

Just a few years ago, it took many, many people to publish a travel flier. People worked for years to learn how to become typesetters, printers, and inkers. Now you can do all these jobs using a computer. You can use desktop publishing to make a travel flier.

Put a check mark next to the item if you think that desktop publishing was used to make it.

- ☐ A photograph of you in front of the Washington Monument
- ☐ The flier placed on your car window advertising a new amusement park
- ☐ A program for the slideshow you saw at Mount Rushmore
- ☐ Handwritten directions your father got from the man at the gas station

36

Terms You Need to Know

THERE are many special words that are used in desktop publishing. You are going to learn four of the most important ones.

See the large words at the top of this page? They catch your attention, don't they? Those words have a special name because they appear at the head of the page or at the beginning of a story. They are called `headlines`.

You want to design your headlines to be eye-catching. That is what makes people want to read further. In different desktop publishing software, headlines are called by different names, but they are basically the same thing.

As you have been reading this page, you have read the next term in desktop publishing: `text`. Text is the words that tell your story. Remember that by using different fonts and point sizes you can make your text look different and more expressive.

Now take a look at the picture on this page. Pictures are called `graphics`. There are many kinds of graphics, including graphs, pictures that you draw, photographs, and `clip art`. Clip art is pictures that you can find on floppy disks.

Show that you understand the terms by writing H for headline, T for text, or G for graphic next to the picture of the travel flier on the left.

37

Designing a Travel Flier

What is desktop publishing?

YOU are going to be visiting many places on your trip across the country. Sitting in the back of the car, you have been looking at the travel fliers of the places you are going to and those you have already visited. Now it's time for you to design your own travel flier.

Designing means laying out the pages. Get a blank piece of 8 1/2-by-11-inch paper. This will be your flier. It will have two pages for you to design. The front is page 1 and the back is page 2. You will design your flier to include the following things.

front page

1. One headline that gives the name of the place or sight-seeing attraction.

2. The text that tells what makes the attraction special.

3. One graphic showing people enjoying this place.

back page

1. One headline as a title for directions to the attraction.

2. The text giving directions to the attraction.

3. One graphic, a map, showing directions to the attraction.

On one page, you might put the text above the graphic. On the other, the text might be below the graphic. These are the decisions a designer would make when creating a travel flier.

On a blank sheet of paper, trace all the shapes on the next page twice. Cut them out and paste them on the front and back of the page you are using for your design layout.

heAdLiNe

grAphic

text

39

Writing a Travel Flier

What is desktop publishing?

Now that you have decided what the flier will look like, it is time to fill in the actual headlines, text, and graphics.

Let's start with the front of the flier. What places do you know about or would you like to learn about? Write some ideas below.

How are you going to describe the place you have chosen? Write some of your ideas below.

Now decide which place you will write about. Put a star next to its name. Then write the name as a headline in the appropriate space on your layout.

When you decide on your final text, copy it in the appropriate space on your layout.

On the back page you have to fill in a headline and text again. The text that you write should be directions to the attraction in your flier. Try writing your directions in the space at the right.

When your directions are clear, copy them and their headline onto the spaces on your layout for page 2.

Graphics for Your Travel Flier

ALL DONE! That was a lot of fun. Let's look at what you've got. Hey wait! There are no pictures. We forgot all about the graphics. Back to the drawing board.

You have two graphic spaces, one on each page of your travel flier. Graphics can be original pictures that you draw or clip art. Clip art is a collection of graphics that you can find in books or on floppy disks. Clip art can be cut or traced out of books and put into your publication.

Now your job is to fill the graphic spaces in the flier. On page 1, you will use clip art or an original drawing. On page 2, you need a graphic of a map. You may use a map you draw yourself or find a map to cut out from a magazine or a book. Please remember that your graphics <u>must</u> fit into the graphic spaces on your design page.

If your flier was about the Pennsylvania Amish Country, you might look for pictures of children riding in horse-drawn carriages, or tables filled with shoofly pie and apple pandowdy. Write a picture idea for an attraction or area of each state below.

1. Texas: _____
_____
2. Florida: _____
_____
3. Oregon: _____
_____
4. Rhode Island: _____
_____
5. Minnesota: _____
_____

what is desktop publishing?

You may want to draw some original computer pictures for the graphic spaces in your travel flier. But how can you do this? You can't draw with crayons or paint on a computer.

You're right. But you have other tools you can use for creating artwork on a computer. In fact, did you know that most of your favorite cartoons are drawn on computer? Drawings on a computer are made up of hundreds of dots called **pixels**. It is like a color-by-number drawing.

Here is a picture that you can color in now.

① blue
② purple
③ red
④ light green
⑤ dark green

Drawing Tools

ARTISTS use different tools to create different effects. Some artists use spray paint, while others use thin brushes or charcoal pencils. These tools and more are yours when you create art on a computer.

The tools are shown on the screen in little pictures called `icons`. You use the mouse to select and use tools. Here is a list of drawing icons and their effect.

- fills the screen or a shape with a color you choose.
- lets you make different types of brush strokes. 
- erases part or all of the picture. 
- lets you make perfect circles. 
- lets you make perfect squares. 
- lets you draw straight lines. 

Look at the postcard below. Then fill in the drawing tool that was used to create each area.

1. truck _____
2. tires _____
3. mountains _____
4. sky _____
5. clouds _____
6. cactus _____

Now that you understand how to use some of the drawing tools that are available, you can create some original artwork for your travel brochure. Have fun!

Resizing Text and Graphics
what is desktop publishing?

SOMETIMES, when you fill in the actual headlines, text, and graphics, you may misjudge the space you have to fill. The picture you used may be much too small to look good in the graphic space that you designed. Or the headline you created may be too large for its space. Do you think you have to start designing your layout page again? NO WAY. You can `resize` it. Resizing doesn't delete or insert anything into the graphic or text. Resizing lets you make headlines, text, or graphics larger or smaller to fit better into your design layout.

Here are some groups of headlines and graphics. Some are the same, but have been resized. Circle the headline or graphic in each group that is resized.

VACATION

NEW YORK

VACATION

VACATION

BON VOYAGE!

GOOD LUCK!
BON VOYAGE!

BON VOYAGE!

44

Word Jumbles

Unscramble the following word jumbles to make words or phrases about desktop publishing. Then use each word or phrase in a sentence.

1 rhaicgp   ___ ___ ___ ___ ___ ___ ___

_____

2 ehedlani   ___ ___ ___ ___ ___ ___ ___ ___

_____

3 ettx   ___ ___ ___ ___

_____

4 zseeri   ___ ___ ___ ___ ___ ___

_____

5 pcrtlia   ___ ___ ___ ___   ___ ___ ___

_____

6 expli   ___ ___ ___ ___ ___

_____

7 sinco   ___ ___ ___ ___ ___

_____

45

What is a Database?

DATABASE software is a computer tool that helps you to organize and store your data. You start getting organized by making lists of things.

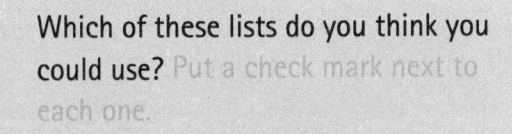

Which of these lists do you think you could use? Put a check mark next to each one.

☐ Names and addresses of friends you want to write letters to

☐ Titles of books you want to read on your trip

☐ Computer games that you play or own

☐ Sights that you want to be sure to see on your trip

☐ Games to play in the car

What are some other lists you might make?
_____
_____

Many people use databases in their work. Look at the workers listed below. Write the type of information each person might put in a database.

Video store manager

_____

_____

Librarian

_____

_____

Doctor

_____

_____

Telephone Operator

_____

_____

Bus Ticket Agent

_____

_____

Hotel Reservation Clerk

_____

_____

Database software uses files to organize information.

So, as you begin this section on databases, keep a picture of a file cabinet in your mind. These are the three components of a database that you will be working with:

❶ A `field` is the smallest item of information in a database.

❷ A `record` is a collection of related fields.

❸ A `file` is a collection of related records.

What if you had to plan a cross-country trip? Where would you start? Let's use our database to organize a pretend cross-country trip.

47

What is a database?

Using Fields to Plan Your Trip

IF YOU were planning a trip, you would need to get organized. There are so many things to decide. Where do you want to go? When will you go and how long will you be gone? Will you take clothing for warm or cold weather?

You can start getting organized by making lists. Where and when are you going? Here are some suggestions: Disneyland, the Statue of Liberty, the Grand Canyon, the Alamo, and Disney World. Let's say you will go in January when you are on winter vacation break.

Let's create a database file to help you plan your trip. The file name will be TRIP. The field names will be PLACE TO VISIT, STATE, TYPE OF PLACE, and AVG. JAN. TEMP.

Draw lines to connect each PLACE TO VISIT field to the STATE, TYPE OF PLACE, and AVG. JAN. TEMP. that describe it.

place to visit
DISNEYLAND
STATUE OF LIBERTY
ALAMO
GRAND CANYON
DISNEY WORLD

state	type of place	avg. jan. temp.
TEXAS	U.S. LANDMARK	53°
ARIZONA	NATIONAL PARK	36°
FLORIDA	AMUSEMENT PARK	61°
CALIFORNIA	AMUSEMENT PARK	58°
NEW YORK	NATIONAL MONUMENT	36°

Now that all the fields are connected, you have created five records. Each row is a record.

Adding Fields to a Record

Here are some field names and some data you might enter if you were planning to visit the White House.

FIELD names must be unique. This means that no two field names can be the same.

city or town	length of stay	kind of lodging
Washington, D. C.	3 days	hotel

Now it's your turn. For each Place listed below, enter data into each new field. Find the city or town the place is in or near. Decide how long you want to stay and whether you will stay in a hotel, motel, inn, or campground. You can have the same data in more than one record.

place to visit	city or town	length of stay	kind of lodging
ALAMO			
GRAND CANYON			
DISNEY WORLD			
DISNEYLAND			
STATUE OF LIBERTY			
MOUNT RUSHMORE			
PIKES PEAK			
GATEWAY ARCH			
CRATER LAKE			

49

What is a database?

Records in a File

LABEL a manila file folder "TRIP." This is your file. There are four Trip Record Cards below. Each record card has seven fields. **Copy these four records onto index cards.** Can you make the five record cards for the PLACES TO VISIT that are missing? Remember to use the same field names. This will be your database file.

trip
PLACE TO VISIT: Disneyland
STATE: California
CITY OR TOWN: Anaheim
AVG. JAN. TEMP.: 58°
TYPE OF PLACE: Amusement Park
LENGTH OF STAY: 2 days
KIND OF LODGING: motel

trip
PLACE TO VISIT: Disney World
STATE: Florida
CITY OR TOWN: Orlando
AVG. JAN. TEMP.: 61°
TYPE OF PLACE: Amusement Park
LENGTH OF STAY: 3 days
KIND OF LODGING: inn

trip
PLACE TO VISIT: Statue of Liberty
STATE: New York
CITY OR TOWN: New York
AVG. JAN. TEMP.: 36°
TYPE OF PLACE: National Monument
LENGTH OF STAY: 1 day
KIND OF LODGING: hotel

trip
PLACE TO VISIT: Grand Canyon
STATE: Arizona
CITY OR TOWN: Grand Canyon Village
AVG. JAN. TEMP.: 36°
TYPE OF PLACE: National Park
LENGTH OF STAY: 2 days
KIND OF LODGING: campground

Now you have nine records in your TRIP file. Next, you will learn how to sort your data.

Sorting by Letter

You can also put your database file in order. The most common way to sort is called **ascending alphabetical order**. That is a fancy way of saying ABC order, which you have been doing for years.

WHEN your class gets in line to move through the halls, your teacher might say, "Line up in size order." Your teacher is sorting the class. The smallest kids go first, and as you look down the line the kids get taller.

Here is a list of words that need to be sorted in ascending alphabetical order. Go to it!

car _____
travel _____
adventure _____
state _____
city _____
train _____
airplane _____
hotel _____
camping _____
lodge _____

When you put fields in order with the letter Z first, then Y, X, W ... that is called **descending alphabetical order**. It is just the opposite of ascending alphabetical order. Now put this list of words in descending alphabetical order.

z y x w v u t s r q p o N M L k j i H g f e d c b a

gasoline _____
restaurant _____
tent _____
hiking _____
suitcase _____
home _____
tourist _____
zoo _____
monument _____
park _____

Wow! You are a Wiz

Now that you know you can sort words, let's get your TRIP file into order. Sort your records into ascending alphabetical order according to the CITY OR TOWN field.

51

What is a database?

Sorting by Number

SOMETIMES, you may have numbers as data in your database file. As a matter of fact, you do. The AVG. JAN. TEMP. field has numbers. When a field has numbers, you can sort from smallest to largest: 1, 2, 3, ... and so on. This is called ascending numerical order. You can probably figure out what sorting numbers in descending numerical order means—ordering the numbers from largest to smallest: 10, 9, 8, and so on.

Here is a chance for you to practice sorting numbers. Put the numbers in Column A in ascending numerical order and the numbers in Column B in descending numerical order.

good Luck!

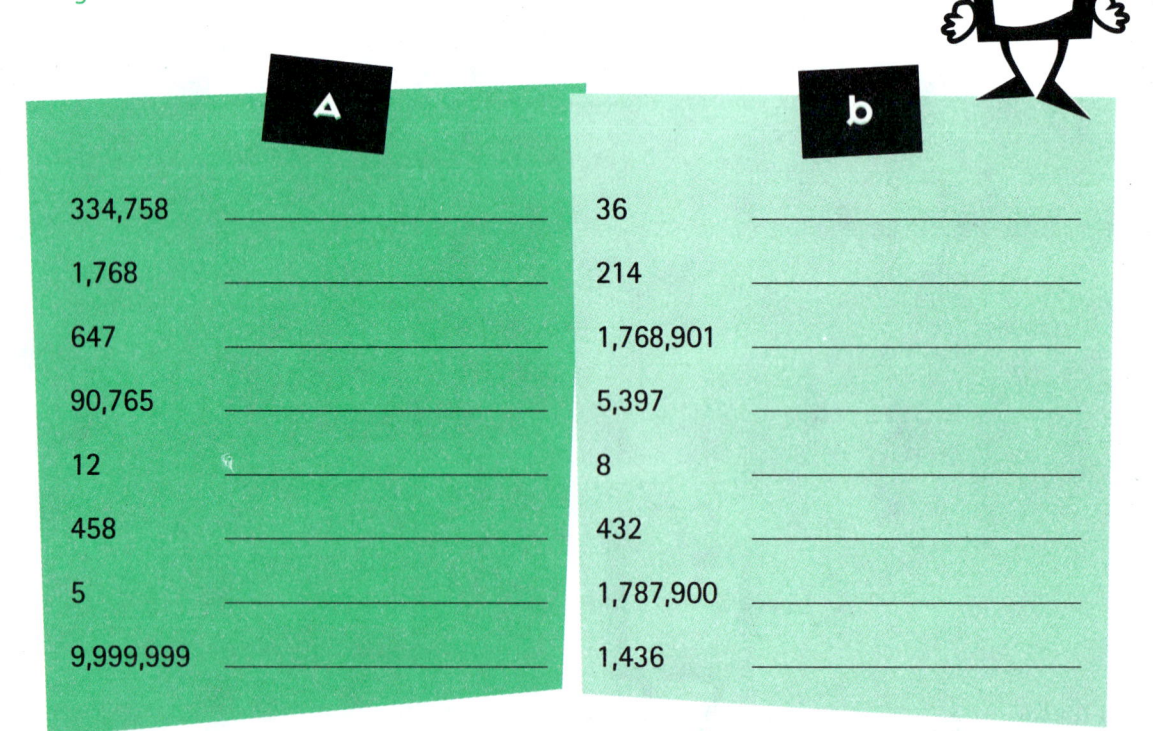

A

334,758	_____
1,768	_____
647	_____
90,765	_____
12	_____
458	_____
5	_____
9,999,999	_____

b

36	_____
214	_____
1,768,901	_____
5,397	_____
8	_____
432	_____
1,787,900	_____
1,436	_____

Queries

QUERY sounds like the word *question*. When you make a query, you are asking the database a question.

How many queries can you think of? Write them in the space. Follow the example:

1. How many states will I visit?
2. _____
3. _____
4. _____
5. _____
6. _____

Using your TRIP database file, answer the following questions.

1. How many records have an average January temperature between 50 and 60 degrees? ☐

2. How many places are you going to visit for more than three days? ☐

3. How many national parks are you going to visit? ☐ How many amusement parks? ☐ How many landmarks? ☐

4. At which places are you going to camp out? ☐

Having all the data entered into your database makes these questions much easier to answer. Imagine if, instead of 9 records in your file, you had 200. It would take a very long time for you to answer these questions if you had to do it yourself. It's a good thing there are database programs!

53

Choose and Use

lists   field   one

ascending   records   Alaska

numerical   organize   question

Chicago   names   alphabetical

Choosing from the words at the left, fill in the blanks to complete the sentences below.

1. Database software is a computer tool that helps you _____ and retrieve data.

2. The smallest item of information in a database is a _____.

3. A file is a collection of _____ that have something in common.

4. One way to get organized is to start making _____.

5. When fields are sorted in ABC order, they are in _____ alphabetical order.

6. Under the field name STATE, you might find _____.

7. These numbers are in descending _____ order: 5, 4, 3, 2, 1.

8. A query is like a _____.

9. A teacher might use a database to list the _____ of the students in the class.

10. A database file can contain hundreds of records or only _____.

What is a Spreadsheet

What is the difference between numbers and numerical data? The number 55 does not mean very much because it is just a number. By adding the description "hotel room costs $55 per night," you get data.

You are going to use a spreadsheet to make a budget for your vacation. Your family will be spending money for lodging, for food, for gasoline, for entrance fees to amusement parks and attractions, and for souvenirs. Spreadsheets are very useful for working out budgets. A budget will help you plan how much money you will need to take with you on your vacation trip.

A SPREADSHEET is a computer software tool used to help analyze numerical data. But what does that mean? With a spreadsheet you can add, subtract, multiply, and divide numbers. You can use formulas to discover information about your data. You can make graphs to see your numbers as pictures.

Below is a list of things you may want on your trip. Put a check mark next to each item that you will need to spend money on.

- Food
- Good weather
- Hotel rooms
- Souvenirs
- Film/Cameras
- Good friends

good work!

Spreadsheets cannot figure out which friends to bring. Spreadsheets cannot guarantee good weather. Spreadsheets **can** tell you how much money you can spend for food and hotels if you want to have money left over to buy souvenirs.

What is a spreadsheet?

You have to plan before you make your budget. Pretend you are planning your dream vacation as you answer each question.

1. For how many days are you planning to travel?..........
2. What is the average cost of a hotel each night?.............
3. How much money will you spend on hotels during the trip?
4. Do you have to rent a car? ....
5. How much does it cost to rent a car each day? ....
6. Are you going to any places that charge entrance fees?.....
7. Approximately how much will each place cost? ....
8. How much do you think you'll spend each day for food? ....
9. Do you have a camera?............
   Will you have to buy film?......
10. How much do you want to spend on souvenirs?................
11. Do you have to buy maps, brochures, or books?...............

A simple spreadsheet that will plan your budget for your trip might look like this. **Figure out the total.**

	A	B
1	Car rental	$30
2	Hotel rooms	$150
3	Food	$65
4	Film/Cameras	$10
5	Souvenirs	$10
6	Maps/Brochures	$15
7	Entrance fees	$100
8	TOTAL:	

If you had $500 to spend, would you have any money left?

A spreadsheet program can add these numbers instantly and do a whole lot more calculating for you.

But, wait! Are these costs for one day or for one week? If you are trying to figure out the cost of a week-long trip, you need to change some figures. One item you need to change is listed below. **Write down the two other items in the list above that you think are daily expenses.**

1. car rental
2. _____
3. _____

Now that you know the data you want to analyze, you can learn how a spreadsheet works.

The Worksheet

A SPREADSHEET program uses a `worksheet` to organize data. The worksheet is made up of `rows` and `columns`.

Rows go across, like this:

Columns go up and down like this:

When the rows and columns are placed on top of each other, a grid is formed. The worksheet grid in a spreadsheet program is just like a tic-tac-toe grid.

Play a quick game of tic-tac-toe with a friend.

Each box that is formed when a row crosses a column is called a cell. In tic-tac-toe you put Xs and Os in the cells.

What do you think you put in the cells in a worksheet?

_____

and _____

Quick thinking! You put numbers and words into the cells in a worksheet

In spreadsheets, words are called `labels`. When you put numbers in cells, they are called `values`. The labels tell you what the values mean.

57

What is a spreadsheet?

Here is a worksheet to plan the budget for your trip.

	A			
1	COST OF	EACH DAY	DAYS	TOTAL
	Car rental	$30	10	$300
	Hotel rooms	$150	10	$1,500
	Food	$65	10	$650
	Entrance fees			$200
	TOTAL			

Each column of a worksheet has a letter at the top. The first column is labeled A. The second column is labeled B. Each row has a number at the left side of the worksheet. The first row is row 1, the second row is row 2, and so on.

1 Put the missing column letters and row numbers in the boxes on the worksheet.

2 How many rows does the worksheet have? ....

How many columns does it have? ....

A spreadsheet can easily calculate those things that you will have to pay for each day.

3 Add up column B to find out the total for each day. Write the total in the total cell for column B.

4 Add up column D to find out the total for the whole trip. Write that total in the total cell for column D.

5 Would you add up the total in column C?

Why or why not?

56

Cell Addresses

When you are working with spreadsheets, you will use the cell address to find the data you need. Let's practice. The first one is done for you.

YOU just learned that columns are lettered and rows are numbered. The **cell address** is made up of the column letter and the row number put together. Cell addresses look like this: A5, B12, C19, ZZ100.

	Cell Address	is for column	and row
1	A1	A	1
2	B12		
3	Z100		
4	FF25		
5	L256		

Now use the cell addresses to answer questions about this worksheet.

	A	B	C	D
1	COST OF	EACH DAY	DAYS	TOTAL
2	Car rental	$30	10	$300
3	Hotel rooms	$150	10	$1,500
4	Food	$65	10	$650
5	Entrance fees			$200
6	Film/Cameras			$10
7	Souvenirs			$50
8	Maps/Brochures/Books			$15
9	TOTAL EXPENSES	$245		$2,725

1 Which cell has the cost of a car rental for each day? ....

2 Which cell has the total cost for car rental? ....

3 Which cell has the number of days you are renting a car? ....

4 Which cell has the word "Food"?

5 Which cell has the words "Entrance fees"? ....

6 Which cell has the cost of maps/brochures/books? ....

7 Which cell has the total for the whole trip?

8 Which cell has the total daily expenses?

9 For how many days are you traveling?

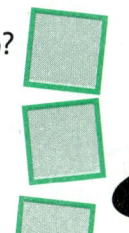

59

What if...?

What is a spreadsheet?

THE power of spreadsheets is being able to ask a *What if?* question. Let's do that now. Go back to your spreadsheet on page 59.

Here is one *What if?* question:

What if we spend $5.00 a day less on food? How much more money would we have to spend on souvenirs?

Can you think of four more *What if?* questions to plan your budget?

1 _____

2 _____

3 _____

4 _____

········· formulas ·········

Spreadsheets use formulas to add, subtract, multiply, or divide values in cells to figure out totals.

Match each math operation to its sign:

addition	×
subtraction	+
multiplication	÷
division	−

Spreadsheets use these symbols: + (add), - (subtract), * (multiply), / (divide). Did you notice that the computer symbols for addition and subtraction are the same as when you write a math formula yourself, but the symbols for multiplication and division are different? In the empty box write the computer symbols for the following formulas:

1 7 ☐ 3 = 10   **3** 3 ☐ 2 = 1

2 4 ☐ 2 = 8   **4** 6 ☐ 2 = 3

60

Draw a line to connect each spreadsheet formula to its description.

Formula	Description
A1 + B1 + C1	Subtract the value in cell D2 from the value in cell C5
A1 * C2	Divide the value in cell A9 by the value in cell D7
C5 - D2	Multiply the value in cell A1 by the value in cell C2
A9/D7	Add the values in cells A1 and B1 and C1

Here is your trip budget worksheet again. Only this time, you can see the formulas that were used to get the answers.

Your trip budget spreadsheet uses many formulas. **Explain what each formula figures out.** (The first one is done for you.)

1. B2+B3+B4
   Total expenses for each day.

2. D2+D3+D4+D5+D6+D7+D8
   _____

3. D10-D9
   _____

4. B4*C4
   _____

5. B3*C3
   _____

	A COST OF	B EACH DAY	C DAYS	D TOTAL
1	COST OF	EACH DAY	DAYS	TOTAL
2	Car rental	$30	10	B2*C2
3	Hotel rooms	$150	10	B3*C3
4	Food	$65	10	B4*C4
5	Entrance fees			$200
6	Film/Cameras			$10
7	Souvenirs			$50
8	Maps/Brochures/Books			$15
9	TOTAL EXPENSES	B2+B3+B4		D2+D3+D4+D5+D6+D7+D8
10	MONEY BROUGHT			$3,000
11	MONEY LEFT			D10-D9

What is a spreadsheet?

Functions

REMEMBER how you calculated the total expenses for each day? You used the formula B2+B3+B4. Keying in all those cell addresses can take a long time, and you could make mistakes. Imagine if you had to add up all the cells in 100 rows! Spreadsheets have built-in formulas that do all types of calculations automatically. These are called functions.

Different spreadsheets have different ways of keying in the functions. But basically, they are all quite similar.

Instead of keying in B2+B3+B4, you can key in SUM(B2..B4). This tells your spreadsheet to find the SUM (or add up) all the cells from B2 to B4.

The AVG or AVERAGE function will find the average value in a group of cells. Let's say you kept track of how much money you spent each day in cells F10 through F20. To find the average you spent each day, you would add up the values in all those cells and divide by 10. You would have to key in:

(F10+F11+F12+F13+F14+F15+F16+F17+F18+F19+F20)/10

The function AVG(F10..F20) in a spreadsheet could figure out the same thing — the average amount you spent each day during your vacation.

As you can see, the SUM function is good for finding totals

What else could you use the AVG function for?

_____

_____

Data as Pictures: Graphing

SPREADSHEETS let you see your numerical data as pictures. Spreadsheets can create pie charts, bar graphs, and line graphs. Pie charts make your data look like a pie. Bar graphs make your data look like bars. Line graphs make your data look like lines.

You can make a bar graph to show the total cost for car rental, hotels, and food on your trip. The graph has been started. Use the figures below to complete it.

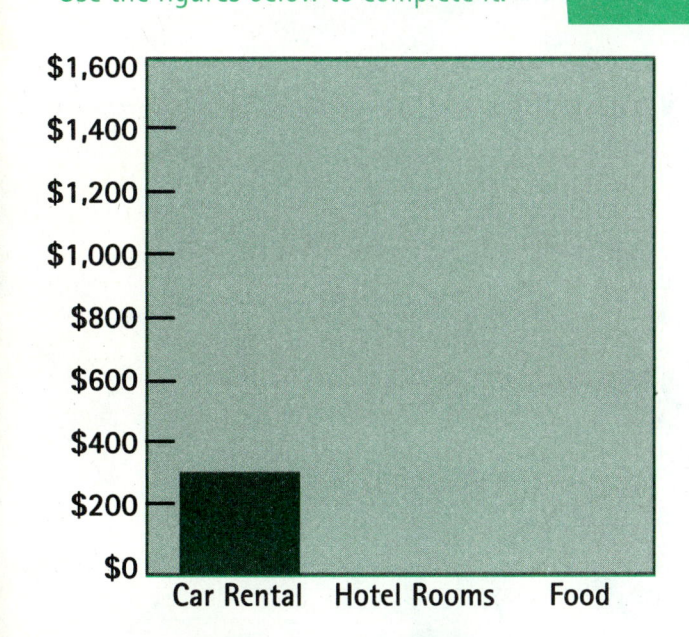

	A	D
1	COST OF	TOTAL
2	Car rental	$300
3	Hotel rooms	$1,500
4	Food	$650
5	TOTAL	$2,450

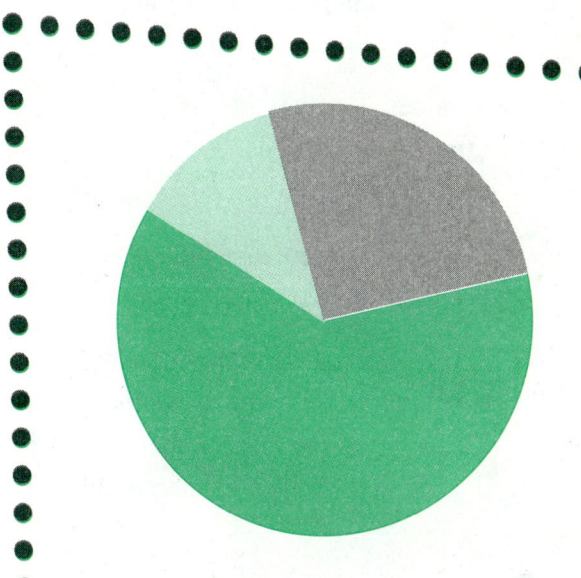

Here is the pie chart. Which slices do you think are for the car, food, and hotels? Write the words on the correct slices.

63

Spread the Answers

Circle the letter of the correct answer or write in your answer.

1 The computer software tool that helps you analyze numerical data is a _____ .

  a. bedspread   c. word processor
  b. spreadsheet   d. calculator

2 The words in a spreadsheet are called _____ .

  a. values   c. data
  b. words   d. labels

3 Cell addresses are made up of the _____ .

  a. row letter and column number
  b. column letter and row number
  c. row letter and row number
  d. column letter and column number

4 The spreadsheet formula A1*B2 means _____ .

  a. add the value in cell A1 to the value in cell B2
  b. multiply the value in cell A1 by the value in cell B2
  c. put a star in cell B2
  d. fill the cells A1 and B2 with asterisks

5 Instead of keying in A1+A2+A3+A4+A5+A6, you can key in _____ .

  a. SUM(A1..A6)   c. (A1+A2+A3+A4+A5+A6)
  b. ALL(A1..A6)   d. addemup(A1+A6)

6 Which of these is NOT a graph type? _____

  a. bubble   c. line
  b. bar   d. pie

7 Why would you use a graph in a worksheet?

  _____
  _____
  _____

64